Introduction

CW00431320

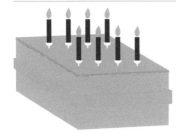

If you have ever wo
legally old enough to have a body piercing,
drink alcohol or get a part-time job, this Guide
is for you. It covers all aspects of age-based
legislation in a systematic and engaging way,
which will appeal to professionals, parents
and children alike.

At What Age Can I...? is produced by
experienced legal professionals at the Children's
Legal Centre and is one of a series of legal guides,
covering issues such as bullying, the police
and confidentiality.

The Children's Legal Centre is a national charity
committed to promoting the rights of children
and young people in the UK and worldwide.
It provides free information, advice and legal
representation to children, young people and
parents on education and child law issues.

At any age

1. s.145 *Licensing Act* 2003.
2. *Confiscation of Alcohol (Young Persons) Act 1997.*

Alcohol

You may enter a bar at any age in the company of a person over the age of 18[1].

The police may confiscate alcohol from you if you are drinking in a public place or any place that you have entered unlawfully. They may also confiscate alcohol from anyone who intends to give you alcohol to drink[2].

Baby-sitting

You can baby-sit for a child at any age, although the parents may wish to assess your suitability to do so. The NSPCC recommends 16 as the minimum age for baby-sitting.

Body Piercing

You can have your body pierced, although your parents may have to accompany you and provide consent.

3. s.8 *Children Act* 1989.
4 ss.13 and 33(7) *Children Act* 1989.

Change of Name

Your parents can change your name without your consent, but you can seek a prohibited steps order from the court if you object[3].

If you want to change your name, you will need the consent of every person with parental responsibility for you[4]. If your parents refuse, you will need to make an application to the court. The court will take your maturity, your reason for changing your name and the implications of such a change into account. Once permission is granted, a change of name can be carried out either by statutory declaration, by simply using a different name and telling everyone you wish to be called by that name, or by deed poll enrolled at the High Court, although you will need to be 16 to enrol a deed poll on your own behalf.

5. *Ryder v Wombell [1868] LR 4 Ex Ch 32, 38.*
6. *De Francesco v Barnum [1889] 43 Ch D 165.*
7. *s.3 Minors' Contracts Act 1987.*

Contracts

Generally, if you are under 18 you cannot enter into contracts. Contracts are legally binding agreements where something valuable is exchanged in return for money. However, you can make valid contracts for 'necessaries' – for example, food or clothing[5]. Motorbikes and stereos would not be considered 'necessaries'. You are bound by such a contract if, on the whole, it is for your benefit[6]. You can also be bound by a contract of employment if it is for your benefit. If you enter into an unenforceable contract and you refuse to pay, the court may order you to return any goods or property received[7].

8. *Race Relations Act 1976.*
9. *Sex Discrimination Act 1975.*
10. *Police Reform Act 2002.*

Discrimination

You can make a complaint if you believe you are discriminated against on the basis of race, colour, ethnic or national origin, or nationality[8], or on grounds of sex or marital status[9]. You can also make a complaint about the police[10].

Film Classifications

You can see a U or PG category film at a cinema unaccompanied by an adult, although the cinema manager has complete discretion over your admission. However, parents are advised to consider whether or not a PG film is suitable for younger children before allowing them to view it. You can buy or rent a U or PG category video, although this is at the discretion of the shopkeeper. You can see a 12A category film at the cinema provided you are accompanied by an adult.

Flying

You can take flying lessons at any age. However, your time will not be recorded until you are 14 years old.

11. s.20(6) *Gaming Act 1968. The Gaming Act 1968* will be repealed by the *Gambling Act 2005* which is not in force yet. The relevant provision will be s. 49 *Gambling Act 2005.*

Gambling

You can enter a bingo club as long as you do not take part in the game[11].

12. *Data Protection Act 1998, Data Protection (Subject Access Modification) (Health) Order 2000, and Data Protection (Subject Access Modification) (Education) Order 2000.*
13. *Data Protection (Subject Access Modification) (Social Work) Order 2000.*

Getting Information

You can ask to see your health records and education records, but you may be refused if to show you might cause serious harm to your physical or mental health, or that of another person[12].

You may also have access to information held by the local authority unless such disclosure would cause serious harm to your physical or mental health, or that of another person. If information is withheld, you can apply to the head of children's services at your local authority, or the chief executive of the council for its release. If you cannot get access, you can apply to the Data Protection Commissioner[13].

Housing

You cannot be a tenant of your own home under the age of 18. Neither can you own property (i.e. land or house) until you are 18, although it can be held in trust for you.

14. s.31 *Children Act 1989.*
15. s.11 *Crime and Disorder Act 1998.*
16. s.14 *Crime and Disorder Act 1998.*
17. s.1 *Children and Young Persons Act 1933.*
18. s.58 *Children Act 2004.*

Legal Issues

Crime

Although you cannot be convicted of a criminal offence under the age of 10, if it is thought that you are suffering, or at risk of suffering, significant harm, and that you are beyond the control of your parents, a care order may be made over you[14].

If you have committed an act that would be a crime if you were over the age of 10, or you have harassed, alarmed or distressed one or more people (other than those you live with) while under the age of 10, a child safety order can be made by the court. This order will last up to three months or, in exceptional circumstances, 12 months. You will be placed under the supervision of a social worker or member of the youth offending team[15].

If you are under 16, you can be the subject of a local child curfew scheme, banning you from public places (except when accompanied by an adult) between 9pm and 6am[16].

If you are under 16, anyone over 16 looking after you may be committing a criminal offence if they ill-treat, assault, neglect or abandon you so as to cause unnecessary suffering or injury to your physical or mental health[17]. A parent may smack you, but this must be justified and must not be excessive or unreasonable bearing in mind your age, understanding, height and build. Smacking, which causes actual bodily harm (e.g. bruising or grazing), cannot be justified as reasonable punishment[18].

19. s.53 *Youth Justice and Criminal Evidence Act 1999.*
20. s.55 *Youth Justice and Criminal Evidence Act 1999.*
21. Part II *Youth Justice and Criminal Evidence Act 1999.*
22. ss.16-30 *Youth Justice and Criminal Evidence Act 1999.*
23. s.96 *Children Act 1989.*
24. *Regulation 3 Community Legal Service (Financial) Regulations 2000.*
25. *Schedule 1 Part 4 Criminal Defence Service (General) (No2) Regulations 2001.*
26. s.41 *Supreme Court Act 1981.*

Giving evidence

You can give evidence in **criminal** proceedings at any age as long as you understand the questions being asked and can give clear answers[19]. If you are under 14, you will give un-sworn evidence[20]. If you are under the age of 17 or are the victim of a sexual offence, you will generally give your evidence through a video interview. In most cases you will need to go to court to be cross-examined, but you will not have to confront the accused. Normally, you will sit in a room outside the courtroom and give evidence through a live-link TV or behind screens. If you qualify for special measures the prosecution lawyer can ask for you to be cross-examined on video at the same time as you give your evidence[21]. The court will usually order the removal of wigs and gowns. In addition, if you are under 17 or have special needs you can give evidence through an intermediary or use communication aids[22].

You can give evidence in **civil** proceedings at any age. If the court thinks that you do not understand the nature of any oath, you can give un-sworn evidence, provided the court believes you understand the duty to tell the truth and you are of sufficient understanding to justify your evidence being heard[23].

Legal aid

You can apply for legal aid at any age, although if you are starting an action in the civil courts or family courts you may need to take that action through a litigation friend (a person who is interested in your welfare). Legal aid will generally be granted if you do not have more income or capital than the amount set out by Government. You will automatically be granted legal aid, regardless of your means, for certain *Children Act 1989* proceedings (for example, applications for care orders or emergency protection orders)[24]. If you are arrested and held in custody at the police station, you are entitled to receive the free services of the duty solicitor. If you are charged with a criminal offence and have to attend court, you are entitled to the free services of the duty court solicitor at the first hearing.

If the case has to return to court, you should instruct a solicitor to apply for a representation order. You will be eligible for this if the court decides it is in the interests of justice to grant it. This may be because it is a serious case and your liberty is at risk, and if you satisfy the financial means test. Your parents' financial situation may be taken into account if you are under 18[25].

Suing and being sued

You can be sued and you will be responsible for any damages awarded against you. However, you cannot be held responsible for a debt that you owe.

Ward of court

In certain circumstances, you can be made a ward of court until the age of 18. This means that the court makes all the important decisions about your life, rather than your parents or anyone else[26]. This can be done if the court decides it is necessary to *'throw some care around you'.*

27. *Gillick v West Norfolk and Wisbech Area Health Authority [1985] 3 All ER 402.*
28. *Re W (A Minor) (Medical Treatment: A Court's Jurisdiction) [1992] 3 WLR 758.*
29. *Re W (A Minor) (Medical Treatment: A Court's Jurisdiction) [1992] 3 WLR 758.*
30. *ss.38(6), 43(8) and 44(7) Children Act 1989.*

Medical Treatment and Examination

You can **give consent** to surgical, medical (including contraceptive) or dental treatment provided the doctor decides you fully understand what is proposed[27]. Your parents cannot override your decision to consent, but a court might overrule you if it thinks it is in your best interests[28].

Up until the age of 18, your **refusal to consent** to medical treatment can be overridden by someone with parental responsibility and by a court[29].

You can refuse to give consent to a psychiatric or medical examination or other assessment in proceedings for an interim care order, emergency protection order or child assessment order when you are of sufficient understanding to make an informed decision[30].

You have the right to seek advice and counselling once you have the 'maturity' to understand the implications of that request. However, your right to complete confidentiality could be restricted if you are at 'risk of significant harm'.

31. *s.1(b) Minors' Contracts Act 1987.*

Money and Banking

The age at which you can open a bank or building society account varies according to the rules of the particular bank or building society, although most have special accounts for children and young people.

You can borrow money or ask for an overdraft while you are under 18, but, since you are not legally responsible for your debts, it may be difficult to find a lender without a guarantor (someone who agrees to pay the money back if you fail to do so)[31]. The same applies to hire purchase and credit agreements: you will need a guarantor until you are 18 years old.

You can have goods or money left to you in a will, but the will may state that you cannot receive the money until you reach a certain age or get married.

32. s.2 Human Tissue Act 2004 and the Human Tissue Authority Code of Practice-Consent.

Organ Donation

You can consent to the storage and use of your tissue if you are considered to be competent; in other words if you understand the consequences of making such an agreement[32].

33. s.71(2),(3) School Standards and Framework Act 1998.

Religion

You can choose your own religion when you have the maturity to understand the implications of your decision. However, if you are under 18 and follow a religion that may be harmful to you, your parents could ask the court to intervene by making you a ward of court.

Only your parent or guardian can withdraw you from religious assembly and instruction at school. He or she can ask that you attend religious instruction outside school, provided it does not interfere with your attendance at school[33].

34. s.405 Education Act 1996.

Sex Education

Only your parent or guardian can withdraw you from sex education at school[34].

35. The Government is currently considering raising the legal age at which young people can buy cigarettes to 18 years old.
36. s.7 Children and Young Persons Act 1933.

Smoking

You can smoke cigarettes, but you are not allowed to buy them until you are 16[35]. If you are caught smoking by a uniformed police officer or park keeper in any public place when under 16, he or she can seize your tobacco and cigarette papers, but not your pipe or tobacco pouch[36].

37. The Motor Vehicles (Wearing of Seat Belts) (Amendment) Regulations 2006.

Travel

If you travel abroad you will need your own passport.

You must use the correct child restraint when travelling in a motor vehicle[37].

You can be a pillion passenger on a motorbike at any age, provided your crash helmet fits properly and both feet reach the passenger foot rests.

5

At Age 5

38. s.5 Children and Young Persons Act 1933.

Alcohol
You can drink alcohol in private[38].

39. s.8(2) Education Act 1996 and Education (Start of Compulsory School Age) Order 1998.
40. s.7 Education Act 1996.

Education
You become of compulsory school age[39] and your parents must ensure you receive full-time education at school or elsewhere – for example, at home[40].

41. National Rail Conditions of Carriage.

Travel
You have to pay a child's fare on trains[41].

7

At Age 7

Money and Banking
You can open and draw money from a National Savings Account or Trustee Savings Bank Account.

10

At Age 10

42. s.34 *Crime and Disorder Act 1998*.
43. s.1 *Sexual Offences Act 1993*.
44. Relevant sexual offences are contained in Schedule 3 *Sexual Offences Act 2003*.
45. s.82(2) *Sexual Offences Act 2003*.

Legal Issues

Crime

You have full criminal responsibility for your actions and can be convicted of a criminal offence[42].

If you are a boy, the law regards you as capable of committing any sexual offence, including rape[43].

If you are convicted of, or receive a reprimand or final warning for, a sexual offence[44], your name will be placed on the sex offenders register. However, if you were under 18 at the time, registration is for half the time that an adult has his or her name registered[45].

If you are detained by the police, you have the right to:
- have someone informed of your detention (if you are under 17, the police **must** take reasonable steps to inform your parents or guardian);
- consult a solicitor;
- consult the Codes of Practice; and
- have an 'appropriate adult' present when you are interviewed, except in certain limited circumstances (the 'appropriate adult' is normally one of your parents).

If you are detained by the police they have the power, in certain circumstances, to:
- search you, including strip search you, without written parental consent;
- carry out an intimate search – an examination of any body orifice without written parental consent, unless the search is in relation to a drugs offence, (generally in the presence of an 'appropriate adult');
- carry out X-rays and body scans with written parental consent, where there are reasonable grounds to suspect that you have swallowed a Class A drug;
- take a non-intimate body sample from you (for example, nail scrapings, saliva and hair), if the Superintendent has reasonable grounds to believe it will prove or disprove your involvement in a recordable offence and written parental consent has been obtained (in certain circumstances this can be done without parental consent);

46. *Police and Criminal Evidence Act 1984; Codes of Practice 2005.*
47. s.1 *Crime and Disorder Act 1998.*
48. s.16 *Powers of Criminal Courts (Sentencing) Act 2000.*
49. s.37 *Powers of Criminal Courts (Sentencing) Act 2000.*
50. s.40A *Powers of Criminal Courts (Sentencing) Act 2000.*
51. s.60 *Powers of Criminal Courts (Sentencing) Act 2000.*
52. s.63 *Powers of Criminal Courts (Sentencing) Act 2000.*
53. s.69 *Powers of Criminal Courts (Sentencing) Act 2000.*

- take an intimate body sample from you (for example, blood, semen, urine and dental impressions), if the Superintendent has reasonable grounds to believe it will prove or disprove your involvement in a recordable offence and written parental consent has been obtained; and
- take your fingerprints with parental consent[46].

If you harass, or cause alarm or distress to one or more people outside your home, the court may make an anti-social behaviour order (ASBO). This can prohibit you from doing certain acts, such as going into the town centre or near a person's home or shop[47].

If you are convicted of an offence by the Youth Court, depending on the seriousness and nature of the offence, various community sentences can be imposed upon you. These are listed below.

A referral order
If you are a first time offender, you will be referred to the Youth Offender Panel. The Panel will agree a contract with you, which will involve reparation to the victim (such as paying compensation or carrying out unpaid work) and measures to tackle the causes of your offending (such as participating in set activities or staying away from certain places)[48].

A curfew order
This requires you to remain at a certain place at certain hours of the day for a maximum of six months[49].

An exclusion order
This prohibits you from entering certain specified places for a maximum period of three months[50].

An attendance centre order
This requires you to attend at a special centre run by the police, generally at the weekend[51].

A supervision order
This can last up to three years. It may require you to live with a particular person or at a particular place, to meet with a specified person (usually the supervisor), to take part or not take part in set activities, to remain in a particular place between 6pm and 6am, undertake medical treatment, comply with arrangements for education, or to make reparation to a particular person or to the community[52].

An action plan order
This requires you to comply with a plan to address your offending behaviour over a period of three months. This usually consists of an intensive programme of work taking account of your particular offending[53].

54. ss.73 and 74 *Powers of Criminal Courts (Sentencing) Act 2000.*
55. ss.130, 135, 136, 150 *Powers of Criminal Courts (Sentencing) Act 2000.*
56. ss.90, 91 *Powers of Criminal Courts (Sentencing) Act 2000.*
57. ss.1 and 5 *Rehabilitation of Offenders Act 1974.*
58. s.29 *Criminal Justice and Court Services Act 2000.*
59. s.149 *Licensing Act 2003.*

A reparation order

This may be ordered if a supervision order is not made. It requires you to undertake work to make amends for your offending, either for the victim or for the community. You may not be asked to do more than 24 hours work[54].

Other possible orders include an order requiring your parents to take proper care of you and exercise proper control over you for a period of up to three years (your parents can be fined up to £1,000 if you do not comply with the terms of your community sentence); and a compensation order (for whatever amount the court thinks appropriate) or a fine of up to £250. The court will order your parents to pay the fine, unless it is unreasonable to do so[55].

> You can be tried in the Crown Court if you are charged with homicide (including murder, manslaughter and causing death by dangerous driving). If you are convicted of a serious offence, the following sentences can be passed:
> * for manslaughter or other grave crimes defined as offences punishable with imprisonment for 14 years or more, such as rape, robbery or indecent assault, you can be given a custodial sentence over the normal two year maximum if you are under 18 years old;
> * for murder, the court must pass a sentence of detention during Her Majesty's pleasure. This means you will be detained for an indefinite period. When sentencing you, the judge will state the minimum period for which you should be detained[56].

If you are convicted of a criminal offence, you will become a rehabilitated person and your conviction will become spent after a certain specified period of time. However, there are certain crimes that are exempt from rehabilitation[57].

> You may be disqualified from working with children when you are an adult if:
> * you have committed a serious sexual or violent offence against another child under 18;
> * you have received a sentence of more than 12 months; and
> * the court is satisfied you are likely to offend again[58].

You will be guilty of an offence if you buy or attempt to buy alcohol[59].

Money and Banking

Most banks or building societies will allow you to open an account, but this is at the discretion of the manager.

11

At Age 11

60. Conditions of Carriage, Transport for London.

Travel

You must pay a child's fare on the underground in London (before the age of 11 you could travel free when accompanied by an adult after 9.30am on weekdays and on weekends and holidays)[60].

12

At Age 12

61. s.24 *Children and Young Persons Act 1933.*

Dangerous Performances

You can be trained to participate in dangerous performances subject to the grant of a local authority licence[61].

Film Classifications

You can see a 12A category film at the cinema without being accompanied by an adult. You can also rent or buy a 12 category video.

62. s.38(6) *Police and Criminal Evidence Act 1984.*
63. s.23 *Children and Young Persons Act 1969.*
64. s.100 *Powers of Criminal Courts (Sentencing) Act 2000.*
65. s.131 *Criminal Justice and Police Act 2001.*

Legal Issues

If you are arrested, you can be kept in police detention or in local authority accommodation, including secure accommodation[62].

You can be remanded to local authority accommodation, including secure accommodation, if you have committed a violent or sexual offence and certain conditions apply[63].

If you are convicted of an offence for which you could have been imprisoned if you were an adult, a detention and training order can be made. This will only be done if the court is of the opinion that a custodial sentence is essential to protect the public from further offending by you. The maximum term is 24 months. Up to half of the sentence will be spent in secure accommodation[64].

If you are released on bail you may be subject to electronic monitoring[65].

66. s.3 *Pet Animals Act 1951.*

Pets

You can buy a pet[66].

Travel

If you are getting a new passport, it must be signed by you and not your parent.

13

At Age 13

67. s.25 *Children Act 1989, Children (Secure Accommodation) Regulations 1991.*

Secure Accommodation

If you are 'looked after' by a local authority, you can be locked up in a secure unit of a children's home for up to 72 hours, or longer by court order. This may happen if you have a history of running away and you are likely to suffer significant harm as a consequence, or you are likely to injure yourself or others if you are not locked up. Younger children may be locked up in secure units only with the agreement of the Secretary of State for Health. You may also be locked up in schools or hospitals if similar conditions apply[67].

14

At Age 14

68. s.18 *Children and Young Persons Act 1933.*
69. s.20 *Children and Young Persons Act 1933.*

Employment

You can get a part-time job involving 'light work', but there are restrictions – you cannot work for more than two hours on a school day or on a Sunday. You cannot work during school hours, nor can you work before 7am or after 7pm. During the school holidays, you may not work for more than five hours a day, or for more than 25 hours a week[68]. The local authority has the power to make bye-laws and you should check with your local Education Welfare Officer if you are considering taking a part-time job.

If local bye-laws allow, you can work for your parents on a weekday as a street trader[69].

70. s.1 *Horses (Protective Headgear for Young Riders) Act 1990.*

Horseriding

You can ride a horse on a road without wearing protective headgear[70].

71. s.135 *Powers of Criminal Courts (Sentencing) Act 2000.*
72. s.161 *Criminal Justice Act 2003.*

Legal Issues

If you are convicted of a criminal offence, you can be fined by the Youth Court up to a maximum of £1,000[71].

If you are convicted of an offence and the court is considering passing a community sentence or a suspended sentence, it may order a drugs test to find out whether there are any specified Class A drugs in your body. The samples must be provided in the presence of an 'appropriate adult'[72].

73. s.25 *Children and Young Persons Act 1933.*

Public Performances

You or your parents may be granted a justices' licence to allow you to take part in public performances abroad. 'Performances' include singing, playing, performing, or being exhibited, for profit, and taking part in a sport or working as a model[73].

74. Conditions of
Carriage, Transport
for London.
75. s.15 *Road Traffic
Act 1988.*

Travel

You must now produce a valid 14-15 Oyster photocard in order to travel free on buses in London[74].

You are now responsible for making sure that you are wearing a seat belt in a car or mini bus if there is one fitted[75].

15

At Age 15

Armed Forces

You can apply to the Royal Navy at 15 years and 9 months.

Film Classifications

You can see a 15 category film at the cinema. You can also rent or buy a 15 category video.

76. s.100 *Powers of
Criminal Courts
(Sentencing) Act 2000.*

Legal Issues

If you are convicted of a crime, other than homicide or a serious crime (see 'At Age 10'), and the offence is so serious that only a custodial sentence is appropriate, or you are a persistent offender (or you will not consent to a community order), you may be sentenced to a detention and training order for a maximum of two years. Half of this time will be spent in a young offenders' institution or other secure accommodation, and half under supervision in the community[76].

16

At Age 16

77. s.54 Anti-social
Behaviour Act 2003.

Aerosol Paint

You can buy aerosol paint[77].

78. ss.145, 149 and
150 Licensing Act 2003.
79. s.149 Licensing
Act 2003.
80. s.148 Licensing
Act 2003.

Alcohol

You can enter a bar on your own, but you can only buy soft drinks. It is a criminal offence to buy, attempt to buy or drink alcohol in licensed premises[78]. However, you may drink beer, cider or wine with a meal if you are accompanied by a person over the age of 18[79].

You can buy liqueur chocolates[80].

Armed Forces

You may join the Army, the Royal Navy, the Royal Air Force and the Royal Marines with parental consent. The armed forces have a minimum service period before you are allowed to leave. For example, if you join the Army but do not like it, you cannot leave in the first 28 days. After that, you can leave on 28 days' notice at any time during the first six months (or, if you are over 18, only during the first three months). After that, you must serve four years.

81. s.4 Children and
Young Persons Act 1933.

Begging

You can be used by another person in order to beg in the street or on any premises[81].

Blood Donation

You can register as a blood donor, but you will not be called to give blood until you are 17 years old.

82. s.3 Children and
Young Persons Act 1933.

Brothels

You are allowed to enter or live in a brothel[82]. You are also allowed to do this under the age of four.

Change of Name

You can change your name by deed poll without parental consent or the consent of the court.

83. s.101 Road Traffic
Act 1988.

Driving

You can hold a licence to drive an invalid carriage or a moped[83]. If you are disabled, you may also hold a licence to drive a car.

84. s.8(3) Education
Act 1996, Education
(School Leaving Date)
Orders 1997.
85. s.2 Learning and
Skills Act 2000.
86. s.63A Employment
Rights Act 1996 and
Right to Time Off for
Study or Training
Regulations 2001.

Education and Training

You can leave school on the last Friday of June either if you are 16 by that date, or you will reach the age of 16 during the summer holidays before the beginning of the next school year[84].

You are still entitled to receive full-time education. Schools, sixth form colleges and city technology colleges are free[85].

You have a right to an offer of a training place if you are not in work or full-time education. If you are in work, and have not reached 'level two' in your training, you have the right to take time off for study or training until you are 17 years old[86].

You may be eligible for Education Maintenance Allowance payments if you continue with your education and fulfil the criteria.

87. s.558 *Education Act 1996.*
88. s.5(1) *Scrap Metal Dealers Act 1964.*

Employment

You can work full-time if you have left school[87], but there are some restrictions on the work you can do. For example, you cannot work in a betting shop or in a bar during opening hours.

You can sell scrap metal[88].

You can join most trade unions at 16; you can join some unions when you are under 16 years old.

Your employer must pay you the national minimum wage set for 16- and 17-year-olds. The national minimum wage changes annually, but you can find the current level on HM Revenue and Customs website (www.hmrc.gov.uk).

89. s.26(2)(b) *Air Navigation Order 2005.*
90. s.37 *Air Navigation Order 2005.*
91. *Schedule 8 Part A Air Navigation Order 2005.*

Flying

You can act as a pilot in command of an aircraft for the purpose of becoming qualified for the grant or renewal of a pilot's licence, or the inclusion or variation of any rating in a pilot's licence[89].

You can act as a pilot in command of a glider[90].

You can hold a flight radiotelephony operator's licence[91].

92. s.21 *Betting, Gaming and Lotteries Act 1963.* This Act will be replaced by the *Gambling Act 2005*, which is not in force yet. The relevant provision will be s.46(2) *Gambling Act 2005.*
93. Regulation 3 *Lotteries Regulations 1993.*

Gambling

You can participate in private or non-commercial gaming or betting, participate in a lottery, football pools and use Category D gaming machines[92]. You can buy a lottery ticket[93].

94. s.15 *Law of Property Act 1925.*
95. ss.175-178 and 188-191 *Housing Act 1996.*
96. *Allocation of Housing Accommodation and Homelessness Guidance.*
97. s.20(3) *Children Act 1989.*
98. s.20(11) *Children Act 1989.*

Housing

You may be able to enter into a contract for housing since this is 'necessary' and the landlord would be able to sue for rent. However, under-18s cannot hold an estate in land, and, therefore, cannot be granted a lease or tenancy, although you could be granted a licence[94].

The local authority has a duty to house you if you are homeless, eligible for assistance, in priority need and did not make yourself intentionally homeless. You may be in priority need if, for example, you are pregnant, have a child or can establish that you are vulnerable[95]. Homeless care leavers and 16- and 17-year-olds will generally be regarded as vulnerable and thus in priority need[96].

The local authority also has a duty to provide you with accommodation if you are in need and your welfare is likely to be 'seriously prejudiced'[97].

You can refuse to be removed from local authority accommodation by your parents or anyone else with parental responsibility[98].

99. s.1(3)(a) *Children Act 1989.*
100. ss.44 and 46 *Children Act 1989.*
101. s.31 *Children Act 1989.*
102. s.3 *Children (Leaving Care) Act 2000.*

Leaving Home

You can probably leave home without the consent of your parents or anyone else with parental responsibility. Any residence order comes to an end at 16 and can only be extended in exceptional circumstances. Wardship proceedings could be brought by your parents for your return home, but the court is unlikely to force you home against your wishes[99]. Where there are serious concerns for your welfare, any person could apply for an emergency protection order or the police could place you in police protection[100]. If you are under 17 years old, the local authority could apply for a care order[101]. It is unlikely that you would be forced to go home in any of those circumstances.

If you are or have been a child 'looked after' by the local authority you will be appointed a personal advisor and a pathway plan will be created to provide you with advice, assistance and support[102].

103. *Regulation 2
Penalties for Disorderly
Behaviour (Form of
Penalty Notice)
Regulations 2002.*
104. *s.177 Criminal
Justice Act 2003.*
105. *s.177(4) Criminal
Justice Act 2003.*

Legal Issues

The Police and Community Support Officers can issue you with an on-the-spot fine (penalty notice)[103].

If you are convicted of a criminal offence, depending on the seriousness of the offence, the court can make the following community orders (in addition to those in 'At Age 10')[104]:

- **an unpaid work requirement:** will require you to perform unpaid work in the community for between 40 and 240 hours;
- **an activity requirement:** will require you to present yourself to a named person at a specific place at a particular time and/or participate in specific activities as set out in the order (these must not exceed 60 days on aggregate);
- **a programme requirement:** will require you to participate in an accredited programme set out in the order at a specified place for a certain number of days;
- **a prohibited activity requirement:** will stop you from participating in specific activities on certain days or for a specific period of time;
- **a residence requirement:** will require you to stay at a certain place for a certain period of time;
- **a mental health requirement:** will require you to receive treatment by or under the direction of a registered medical practitioner or a chartered psychologist (or both) for a certain period of time to try to improve your mental condition;
- **a drug rehabilitation requirement:** if you are believed to be a drug user, will require you to receive treatment for a specified period to try to reduce or eliminate your dependency on drugs, and you may also be required to provide samples to detect whether there are drugs in your body, the order has to be for at least six months; and
- **an alcohol treatment requirement:** if you are believed to be dependent on alcohol, will require you to receive treatment for a specified period of time to try to reduce or eliminate your dependency on alcohol. You will have to show that you are willing to comply with the requirements, the order has to be for at least six months.

When the court has ordered a community service order (above), it may also impose an electronic monitoring requirement (an electronic tag)[105].

You can apply for legal help and assistance at court from the Legal Services Commission: criminal legal aid and civil legal aid. You will be assessed on your own means, even if you are in full-time education or vocational training (see also 'At Any Age').

106. s.3(1) *Marriage Act 1949*. s.4 *Civil Partnership Act 2004*.

Marriage and Civil Partnership

You can marry or register a civil partnership with parental consent. You will need the consent of both parents if they are married. If they are not married, you will only need the consent of your mother, unless your father has parental responsibility for you. If parental consent is refused, a court can authorise the marriage[106].

107. ss.8 and 21(2) *Family Law Reform Act 1969*.
108. Regulation 7 *National Health Service (Charges for Drugs and Appliances) Regulations 2000*.
109. Regulation 8 *National Health Service (Charges for Drugs and Appliances) (Wales) Regulations 2001*.
110. Regulations 3 and 8 *National Health Service (Optical Charges and Payments) Regulations 1997*.

Medical Treatment

You can consent to surgical, medical or dental treatment, including the taking of blood samples (see also 'At Any Age') and also choose your own doctor[107].

If you are female, you can purchase emergency contraception (the 'morning after' pill) over-the-counter in a pharmacy.

You have to pay prescription charges, unless you are in full-time education, pregnant, in receipt of income support, on a low income or in certain other circumstances[108]. In Wales, you do not have to pay prescription charges until you are 25[109]. You have to pay for a sight test and for glasses unless you are in full-time education[110].

Money and Banking

You can buy Premium bonds.

You can open an Individual Savings Account (ISA).

If you are a care leaver you will be entitled to certain benefits.

111. s.37 *Children and Young Persons Act 1963*.

Public Performances

You can take part in public performances without a local authority licence[111].

At What Age Can I...? A guide to age-based legislation

112. ss.9 and 13 *Sexual Offences Act 2003*.
113. As defined by ss.21 and 22 *Sexual Offences Act 2003*.
114. s.16 *Sexual Offences Act 2003*.

Sex

You can consent to all sexual activity (heterosexual and homosexual) involving other males and females aged 16 years and over. Engaging in any sexual activity (from kissing to full penetration) above or below the age of 16 years with another person who is below the age of 16 is a criminal offence, regardless of consent[112].

Anyone who is in a 'position of trust'[113] and who is aged 18 years old or over will commit an offence if he or she engages in any sexual activity with a person below the age of 18[114].

115. s.7 *Children and Young Persons Act 1933*. The Government is currently considering raising the legal age at which young people can buy cigarettes to 18 years old.

Smoking

You can buy cigarettes, tobacco and cigarette papers[115].

116. s.2(2) *Identity Cards Act 2006*.
117. s.124 *Social Security Contributions and Benefits Act 1992* and Schedule 1B Income Support (General) Regulations 1987.
118. s.16 *Jobseekers Act 1995*.
119. s.6 *Children (Leaving Care) Act 2000*.
120. s.24A *Children Act 1989*.

Social Security

You can get a National Insurance Number.

You will be entered on the National Identity Register (which is not yet in force)[116].

You may receive income support in certain circumstances. For example, if you are still in full-time education at school or college and are forced to live away from your parents and they are not keeping you, or you cannot work or take up a training place because you are disabled or have dependent children[117]. You may also be able to obtain a jobseeker's allowance if you are registered for training but you are not receiving any, and you are also suffering severe hardship[118].

If you are an 'eligible' child or a 'relevant' child (you have been 'looked after' by the local authority for at least 13 weeks from the age of 14, whether or not you are still 'looked after' by the local authority), you are excluded from claiming income support, housing benefit or jobseeker's allowance, but you can seek financial assistance from the local authority[119].

If you are a 'qualifying' child (you have been 'looked after' by a private foster carer, in a hospital, registered mental hospital or residential school for a period of at least three months), the local authority may provide assistance in exceptional circumstances[120].

121. *Child Support (Maintenance Calculation and Special Cases) Regulations 2000.*

You may be assessed to pay child support if you are an absent parent, although it is unlikely that such an assessment would be enforced where the absent parent is still under the age of 18 years old (the Child Support Agency, which enforces the payment of child support is currently going through a period of reform and the rules may change)[121].

122. *Conditions of Carriage, Transport for London.*
123. *Conditions of Carriage, Transport for London.*

Travel

You can apply for your own passport, but a parent or person caring for you must give written consent. You do not need parental consent if you are married or in the armed forces.

You have to pay full fare on trains[122] and on buses and the underground in London[123]. You may also have to pay full fare in other areas.

124. s.141A *Criminal Justice Act 1988.*
125. s.43 *Violent Crime Reduction Act 2006.*

Weapons

It is no longer an offence for a shopkeeper to sell you a knife, knife blade, razor, axe or any other article which has a blade or which is sharply pointed and which can be used to cause injury[124]. However, this age is due to rise to 18 under the *Violent Crime Reduction Act 2006*[125].

17

At Age 17

Armed Forces

You can join the Royal Navy or the Royal Marines as an officer with parental consent at 17, the Royal Air Force at 17 years and six months, and the Army at 17 years and nine months.

You can join the Royal Marines Reserve and the Territorial Army with parental consent.

Blood Donation

You can donate blood without parental consent.

126. s.31(3) *Children Act 1989.*

Care Orders

The local authority can no longer apply for a care order for you[126].

127. s.101 *Road Traffic Act 1988.*

Driving

You can hold a licence to drive a car, small goods vehicle and an agricultural tractor on the road, but not a medium or heavy goods vehicle, or a vehicle that carries more than eight passengers[127]. You may now fill up your car with petrol.

Fire Service

You can apply to certain fire bridges at 17 years and 10 months old.

128. *Schedule 8 Part A Air Navigation Order 2005.*

Flying

You can hold a national and private pilot's licence to fly an aeroplane. You can hold a private pilot's licence to fly a helicopter, gyroplane, balloon or an airship[128].

129. s.65 *Crime and Disorder Act 1998.*
130. s.23 *Children and Young Persons Act 1969.*

Legal Issues

You can be given a reprimand or warning without an 'appropriate adult' being present[129].

If you have been charged with an offence and not granted bail, you will be sent to a remand centre or prison[130].

131. s.22(1) *Firearms Act 1968.*
132. s.33(2) *Violent Crime Reduction Act 2006.*
133. ss.22 and 23 *Firearms Act 1968.*
134. s.33(3) *Violent Crime Reduction Act 2006.*
135. ss.2 and 3 *Crossbows Act 1987.*
136. s.44(1) *Violent Crime Reduction Act 2006.*

Weapons

You can buy or hire any firearm or ammunition[131]. This age is due to rise to 18 for the purchase or hire of air weapons or air weapon ammunition, but remain at 17 for firearms or ammunition of other descriptions[132].

You can possess an air weapon under the age of 17, provided you are supervised by someone aged 21 or over, or you are using it at a rifle club or shooting gallery[133]. This age is due to rise to 18 for possession of an air weapon[134].

You can buy or hire a crossbow. Under-17s who have in their possession a crossbow capable of discharging a bolt can be convicted of a criminal offence unless under the supervision of someone aged 21[135]. This age is due to rise to 18 for purchase, hire and possession of a crossbow[136].

18

137. s.1 *Family Law Reform Act 1969.*

At Age 18

You are the age of majority and no longer a child[137].

138. ss.56-64 *Adoption and Children Act 2002.*
139. s.80 *Adoption and Children Act 2002.*

Adoption

You cannot be adopted.

If you have been adopted, you can contact the adoption agency responsible for your adoption for more information, for example, a copy of your original birth certificate[138].

If you have been adopted, you can apply to have your name and address put on the Adoption Contact Register[139].

140. s.146 *Licensing Act 2003.*
141. s.111 *Licensing Act 2003.*

Alcohol

You can buy and drink alcohol in a bar[140].

You can apply for a licence to sell alcohol[141].

Armed Forces

You can join the armed forces and all volunteer reserves (part-time armed forces) without parental consent.

142. s.35 *Finance Act 2005.*
143. s.1(a) *Minors' Contracts Act 1987.*
144. s.114(2) *Consumer Credit Act 1974.*

Contracts and Property Ownership

You have complete contractual capacity, so you can make binding contracts in your own right. You can own land, buy a house or flat, hold a tenancy or apply for a mortgage. You can become entitled to any property that has been held in trust for you[142]. You can act as an executor or administrator of a deceased person's estate. You can ratify an unenforceable contract entered into when you were under 18 years old[143]. You can pawn an article at a pawnshop[144].

145. s.101 *Road Traffic Act 1988.*

Driving

You can hold a licence to drive a medium-sized goods vehicle (maximum 7.5 tonnes)[145].

At What Age Can I...? A guide to age-based legislation

Employment

Your employer must pay you the national minimum wage set for 18-year-olds. This changes annually, you can find out what the current minimum wage is on HM Revenue and Customs website (www.hmrc.gov.uk).

146. *s.7 Video Recordings Act 1984.*

Film Classifications

You can see an 18 category film at the cinema.

You can buy or rent a video given a certificate for viewing by adults only[146].

Fire Service

You can join the fire service at 18 years old.

147. *Regulation 6 Fireworks (Safety) Regulations 1997.*

Fireworks

You can buy fireworks[147].

148. *Schedule 8 Part A Air Navigation Order 2005.*

Flying

You can hold a commercial pilot's licence to fly an aeroplane, helicopter, gyroplane, balloon, airship or glider[148].

149. *s.21 Betting, Gaming and Lotteries Act 1963* and *s.7 Gaming Act 1968.* These Acts will be repealed by the *Gambling Act 2005,* which is not in force yet. The relevant provisions will be ss.46,47,51 *Gambling Act 2005.*

Gambling

You can enter a betting shop and place a bet. You can also work in one. You may enter premises in which gaming takes place[149].

150. s.1 *Gender Recognition Act 2004.*

Gender Change

You can make an application for a gender change certificate if you have been living as the other gender or have changed gender[150].

Leaving Home

You can leave home without parental consent.

151. s.46(1) *Children and Young Persons Act 1933* and s.68 *Criminal Justice Act 1991.*
152. s.1 *Juries Act 1974.*
153. s.7 *Wills Act 1837.*
154. s.1 *Wills (Soldiers and Sailors) Act 1918.*

Legal Issues

Criminal charges against you will be dealt with in the adult courts[151]. You can appear before an adult court.

You can serve on a jury[152].

You can be sued and you can sue in your own right.

You can make a will[153]. If you are in the armed forces or a marine or a seaman, you can make a will when you are under 18[154].

You can make an application for legal aid in your own right (see also 'At Any Age').

155. s.4 *Civil Partnership Act 2004.*

Marriage and Civil Partnership

You can get married without parental consent. You can register a civil partnership without parental consent[155].

156. s.183 *Health and Social Care (Community Health and Standards) Act 2003.*

Medical Treatment

You have to pay for dental treatment unless you are still in full-time education, pregnant or certain other circumstances apply[156].

157. s.1(b) *Minors' Contracts Act 1987.*

Money and Banking

You can agree to pay a loan provided when you were under-18 years old[157].

You can open a bank account or get a credit card without your parents' signature. You are also able to take out a personal loan.

158. *The Police (Minimum Age for Appointment) Regulations 2006.*

Police

You can apply to join the police service and you may be appointed at this time[158].

159. s.1 *Representation of the People Act 2000.*

Political Participation

You can vote in general and local elections[159].

160. s.3 *Hypnotism Act 1952.*

Public Performances

You can take part in an exhibition or performance of hypnotism[160].

161. s.6 *Children (Leaving Care) Act 2000.*

Social Security

You can now claim income support if you have been an 'eligible' or 'relevant' child (see 'At Age 16')[161].

162. s.1 *Tattooing of Minors Act 1969.*

Tattoo

You can be tattooed[162].

Travel

You can apply for a passport without parental consent.

19

At Age 19

163. s.2 *Learning and Skills Act 2000.*

Education

You are entitled to full-time education, up to the age of 19 years old[163].

164. *National Health Service (Charges for Drugs and Appliances) Regulations 2000.*
165. s.183 *Health and Social care (Community Health and Standards) Act 2003.*

Medical Treatment

You have to pay prescription charges[164].

You have to pay for dental treatment even if you are in full-time education[165], but you can apply to be exempt if you have a low income.

21

At Age 21

166. ss.50 and 51 *Adoption and Children Act 2002.*

Adoption

You can adopt a child[166].

167. s.101 *Road Traffic Act 1988.*

Driving

You can supervise a learner driver if you have held, and still hold, a full licence for that type of motor car for at least three years.

You can apply for a provisional licence to drive a large passenger vehicle or heavy goods vehicle[167].

168. *Schedule 8 Part A Air Navigation Order 2005.*

Flying

You can hold an airline transport pilot's licence for an aeroplane, helicopter and gyroplane. You can hold a flight navigator's licence and a flight engineer's licence[168].

169. s.3 *Children (Leaving Care) Act 2000.*
170. s.24 *Children Act 1989.*

Leaving Care

If you are or have been a child 'looked after' by the local authority and you were appointed a personal advisor and a pathway plan was created, these will usually terminate when you are 21 unless you are in further education or training[169].

If you were 'looked after' by the local authority between the ages of 16 and 18, the local authority continues to be under a duty to advise and befriend you. If you are in higher education the local authority has a duty to assist you financially up until the age of 24 if necessary[170].

171. s.7 *Parliamentary Elections Act 1695.*
172. s.79(1) *Local Government Act 1972.*
These ages are due to change to 18, when s.17 *Electoral Administration Act 2006* comes into force.

Political Participation

You can become a Member of Parliament[171], a local councillor or a mayor[172].

Contact Details

The Children's Legal Centre
University of Essex
Wivenhoe Park
Essex CO4 3SQ

Telephone: 01206 872466
Fax: 01206 874026
Email: clc@essex.ac.uk
Website: www.childrenslegalcentre.com

October 2006 © Children's Legal Centre
ISBN: 0 946109478

Designed by Phelan Barker LLP
Printed by Technographic